Piano • Vocal • Guitar

Beautiful Ballads

This publication is not for sale in
the EC and/or Australia
or New Zealand.

ISBN 0-7935-3521-2

HAL•LEONARD
CORPORATION
7777 W. BLUEMOUND RD. P.O. BOX 13819 MILWAUKEE, WI 53213

ALFIE
(Theme From The Paramount Picture "ALFIE")

Words by HAL DAVID
Music by BURT BACHARACH

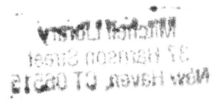

5

ALL THE THINGS YOU ARE

(From "VERY WARM FOR MAY")

Lyrics by OSCAR HAMMERSTEIN II
Music by JEROME KERN

Moderately Slowly

You are the prom-ised kiss of spring-time That makes the lone-ly win-ter seem long. _____

You are the breath-less hush of eve-ning That

ALWAYS ON MY MIND

Words and Music by WAYNE THOMPSON, MARK JAMES
and JOHNNY CHRISTOPHER

AND I LOVE YOU SO

Words and Music by
DON McLEAN

MCA music publishing

AND SO IT GOES

Words and Music by
BILLY JOEL

Slow Ballad, with much rubato

APRIL IN PARIS

Words by E.Y. HARBURG
Music by VERNON DUKE

AUTUMN IN NEW YORK

Words and Music by
VERNON DUKE

Andantino (poco rubato)
mp
Gm
C7
F
p
It's time to end my lone-ly hol - i - day And bid the
poco rit.
p legato
C7
Fm
C
Gm
C7
coun - try a has - ty fare - well. So on this gray and mel - an -
3

BEYOND THE SEA

English Lyrics by JACK LAWRENCE
Music and French Lyrics by CHARLES TRENET

know_____ be-yond a doubt, my heart will lead me there

soon._____ We'll meet_____ be-yond the

shore, we'll kiss just as be-fore,_____ Hap-py we'll

be Be-yond The Sea_____ and nev-er a-gain I'll go

sail - ing. Some - sail - ing._____

BLUE ON BLUE

Lyric by HAL DAVID
Music by BURT BACHARACH

BLESS THE BEASTS AND CHILDREN

Words and Music by BARRY DeVORZON
and PERRY BOTKIN, JR.

Coda

Bless the beasts and the chil - dren; Give them shel -

ter from a storm; Keep them safe;

Keep them warm.

BLUE VELVET

Words and Music by BERNIE WAYNE
and LEE MORRIS

Slowly (with expression)

BORN FREE

(From The Columbia Pictures' Release "BORN FREE")

Words by DON BLACK
Music by JOHN BARRY

where no walls di - vide you,_____ you're free as a

roar - ing tide, so there's no need to hide._____

Born free,_____ and life is worth liv - ing,_____ but on - ly worth

liv - ing 'cause you're born free._____

C'EST SI BON (IT'S SO GOOD)

English Words by JERRY SEELEN
French Words by ANDRE HORNEZ
Music by HENRI BETTI

MCA music publishing

CAN'T HELP FALLING IN LOVE

Words and Music by GEORGE DAVID WEISS,
HUGO PERETTI and LUIGI CREATORE

CALL ME IRRESPONSIBLE

(From The Paramount Picture "PAPA'S DELICATE CONDITION")

Words by
SAMMY CAHN

Words by SAMMY CAHN
Music by JAMES VAN HEUSEN

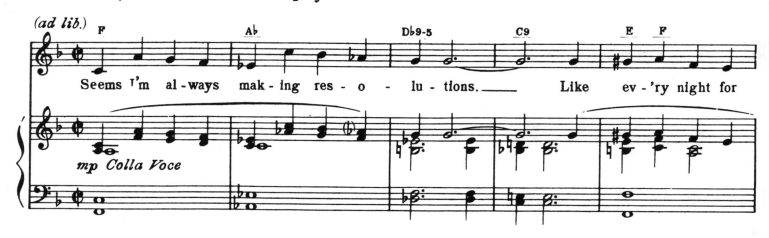

Refrain, Slowly With A Smooth, Steady Rhythm

(THEY LONG TO BE) CLOSE TO YOU

Lyric by HAL DAVID
Music by BURT BACHARACH

COME RAIN OR COME SHINE
(From "ST. LOUIS WOMAN")

Words by JOHNNY MERCER
Music by HAROLD ARLEN

COME SATURDAY MORNING

(a/k/a Saturday Morning)

(From The Paramount Picture "THE STERILE CUCKOO")

Words by DORY PREVIN
Music by FRED KARLIN

Moderato but not too slow

mf

mp

Come Sat-ur-day morn - ing I'm
Come Sat-ur-day morn - ing I'm

go - ing a - way with my friend; We'll
go - ing a - way with my friend; We'll

COULD IT BE MAGIC

Words and Music by
ADRIENNE ANDERSON and BARRY MANILOW

Ba - by I want __ you.

tacet

D. S.al Coda 𝄋

CODA

CRY ME A RIVER

Words and Music by
ARTHUR HAMILTON

DO YOU KNOW WHERE YOU'RE GOING TO?

(Theme From "MAHOGANY")

Words by GERRY GOFFIN
Music by MIKE MASSER

Do you know_____ where you're go-ing to? Do you like the things that life is show-ing you?_____ Where are you go-ing to,_____ do you know?

Why must _ we wait so long _ be - fore we see

how sad the an - swers to those ques - tions can be?_____

know?

DON'T CRY FOR ME ARGENTINA

(From "EVITA")

Words by TIM RICE
Music by ANDREW LLOYD WEBBER

MCA music publishing

all you have to do is look at me to know that ev - 'ry word is true.

EAST OF THE SUN
(And West Of The Moon)

Words and Music by
BROOKS BOWMAN

Slowly , with expression

East of the sun _____ and west of the moon, _____

_____ we'll build a dream-house _____ of love,

dear. Near to the sun in the day,

FOR ALL WE KNOW
(From The Motion Picture "LOVERS AND OTHER STRANGERS")

Words by ROBB WILSON
and JAMES GRIFFIN
Music by FRED KARLIN

Moderato, with a light beat

Love, _____ look at the two of us, _____ Stran-

gers _____ in man-y ways. _____

EVEN NOW

Words by MARTY PANZER
Music by BARRY MANILOW

(I LOVE YOU)
FOR SENTIMENTAL REASONS

Words by DEEK WATSON
Music by WILLIAM BEST

Slowly

I love you _____ for sen-ti-men-tal rea-sons, _____

_____ I hope you do be-lieve me, _____ I'll give you my

HAVE I TOLD YOU LATELY

Words and Music by
VAN MORRISON

GENTLE ON MY MIND

Words and Music by
JOHN HARTFORD

2. It's not clinging to the rocks and ivy planted on their columns now that binds me
Or something that somebody said because they thought we fit together walkin'.
It's just knowing that the world will not be cursing or forgiving when I walk along
Some railroad track and find
That you're moving on the backroads by the rivers of my memory and for hours
You're just gentle on my mind.

3. Though the wheat fields and the clothes lines and junkyards and the highways
Come between us
And some other woman crying to her mother 'cause she turned and I was gone.
I still run in silence, tears of joy might stain my face and summer sun might
Burn me 'til I'm blind
But not to where I cannot see you walkin' on the backroads by the rivers flowing
Gentle on my mind.

4. I dip my cup of soup back from the gurglin' cracklin' caldron in some train yard
My beard a roughning coal pile and a dirty hat pulled low across my face.
Through cupped hands 'round a tin can I pretend I hold you to my breast and find
That you're waving from the backroads by the rivers of my memory ever smilin'
Ever gentle on my mind.

HARBOR LIGHTS

Words and Music by JIMMY KENNEDY
and HUGH WILLIAMS

HERO

Words and Music by MARIAH CAREY
and WALTER AFANASIEFF

105

I DON'T WANT TO WALK WITHOUT YOU

(From The Paramount Picture "SWEATER GIRL")

Words by FRANK LOESSER
Music by JULE STYNE

I LOVE PARIS

(From "CAN CAN")

Words and Music by
COLE PORTER

I WISH YOU LOVE

English Words by ALBERT BEACH
French Words and Music by CHARLES TRENET

I WRITE THE SONGS

Words and Music by
BRUCE JOHNSTON

I've been a- live for- ev-er,___ and I wrote the ver- y first song.___

My home lies deep with- in you___ and I've got my own place in your

soul.

I put the words and the mel- o- dies to- geth- er, I am

Now, when I look out through your eyes___ I'm

mu- sic, and I write the songs.___

young a- gain, e- ven though I'm ver- y old.___

I'LL BE SEEING YOU

(From "RIGHT THIS WAY")

Lyric by IRVING KAHAL
Music by SAMMY FAIN

I'LL NEVER SMILE AGAIN

Words and Music by
RUTH LOWE

I'VE GOT YOU UNDER MY SKIN

Words and Music by
COLE PORTER

I'VE GROWN ACCUSTOMED TO HER FACE

(From "MY FAIR LADY")

Words by ALAN JAY LERNER
Music by FREDERICK LOEWE

IF

Words and Music by
DAVID GATES

Moderately, with feeling

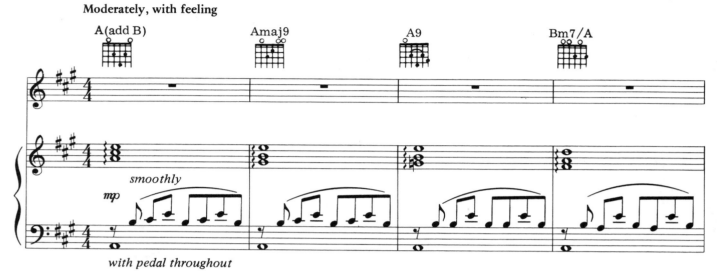

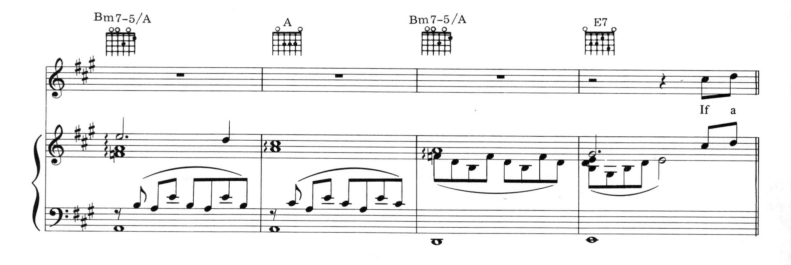

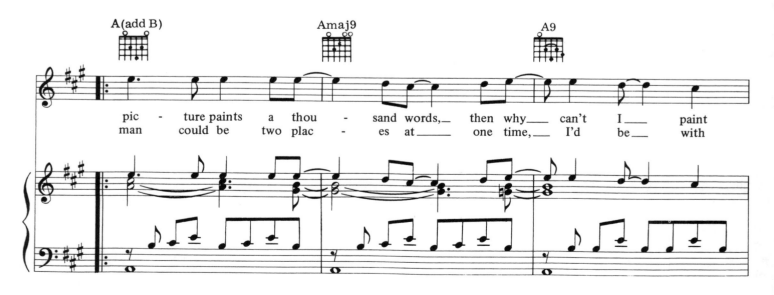

pic - ture paints a thou - sand words,__ then why__ can't I__ paint

man could be two plac - es at__ one time,__ I'd be__ with

IMAGINE

Words and Music by
JOHN LENNON

ISN'T IT ROMANTIC?

(From The Paramount Picture "LOVE ME TONIGHT")

Words by LORENZ HART
Music by RICHARD RODGERS

I've nev-er met you, Yet nev-er doubt, dear, I can't for-
My face is glow-ing, I'm en-er-get-ic, The art of

get you, I've thought you out, dear, I know your pro-file and I know the way you
sew-ing, I found po-et-ic, My nee-dle punc-tu-ates the rhy-thm of ro-

kiss just the thing I miss on a night like this. If dreams are
mance! I don't give a stitch, if I don't get rich. A cus-tom

Fm C7 Fm B♭7 G7 Cm Cm7
Sweet sym - bols in the moon - light, Do you mean that
We'll help the pop - u - la - tion, It's a du - ty
Am7♭5 Fm7♭5 E♭ C♯dim B♭7
I will fall in love per chance? Is - n't it ro -
that we owe to dear old France. Is - n't it ro -
1 E♭ Adim B♭7
mance? Is - n't it ro -
2 E♭ Fm7♭5 E♭
mance?

IT MUST BE HIM
(Original French Title: "Seul Sur Son Etoile")

Words and Music by GILBERT BECAUD
and MAURICE VIDALIN
English Adaptation by MACK DAVID

IT'S EASY TO REMEMBER

(From The Paramount Picture "MISSISSIPPI")

Words by LORENZ HART
Music by RICHARD RODGERS

tight._____ I'd rath-er dream_____ than have that lone-ly feel-ing steal-ing through the

night._____ Each lit-tle mo-ment_____ is clear be-fore me,_____ and though it

brings me re-gret, it's eas-y to re-mem-ber and

so hard to for-get._____ Your sweet ex -   so hard to for-get.

JUNE IN JANUARY
(From The Paramount Picture "HERE IS MY HEART")

Words and Music by LEO ROBIN
and RALPH RAINGER

IT'S IMPOSSIBLE (SOMOS NOVIOS)

English Lyric by SID WAYNE
Spanish Words and Music by
ARMANDO MANZANERO

JUST IN TIME
(From "BELLS ARE RINGING")

Words by BETTY COMDEN
and ADOLPH GREEN
Music by JULE STYNE

JUST ONE MORE CHANCE

Words by SAM COSLOW
Music by ARTHUR JOHNSTON

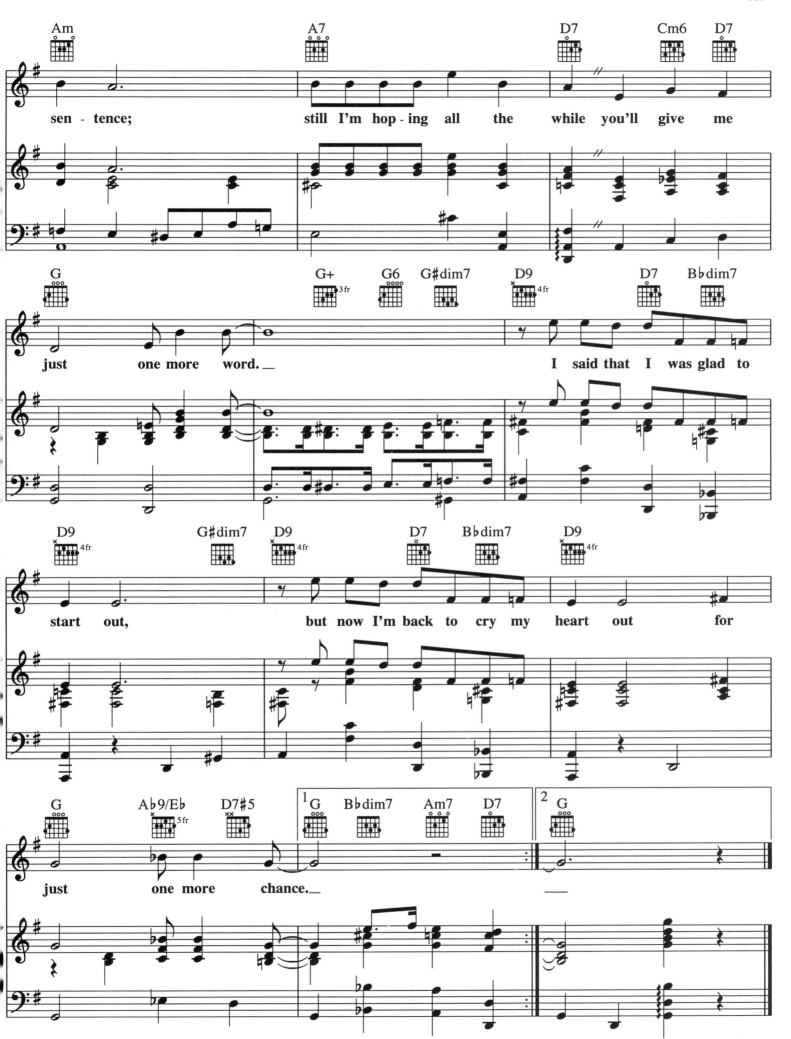

THE LAST TIME I SAW PARIS

Lyrics by OSCAR HAMMERSTEIN II
Music by JEROME KERN

last time I saw Par - is Her heart was warm and gay, I

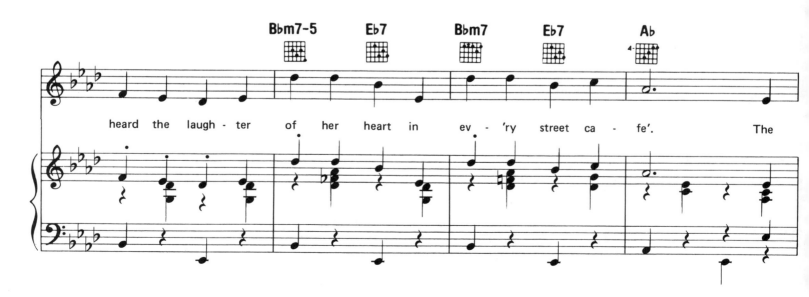

heard the laugh - ter of her heart in ev - 'ry street ca - fe'. The

LONG AGO (AND FAR AWAY)

(From "COVER GIRL")

Words by IRA GERSHWIN
Music by JEROME KERN

LET IT BE ME (JE T'APPARTIENS)

English Words by MANN CURTIS
French Words by PIERRE DeLANOE
Music by GILBERT BECAUD

Relaxed

I bless the day I found you, I want to stay a-round you,
If, for each bit of glad-ness, Some-one must taste of sad-ness,

And so I beg you, let it be me. Don't take this
I'll bear the sor-row, let it be me. No mat-ter

heav-en from one, If you must cling to some-one, Now and for-ev-er,
what the price is, I'll make the sac-ri-fic-es, Through each to-mor-row,

MCA music publishing

LITTLE GIRL BLUE
(From "JUMBO")

Words by LORENZ HART
Music by RICHARD RODGERS

LOLLIPOPS AND ROSES

Words and Music by
TONY VELONA

THE LONG AND WINDING ROAD

Words and Music by JOHN LENNON
and PAUL McCARTNEY

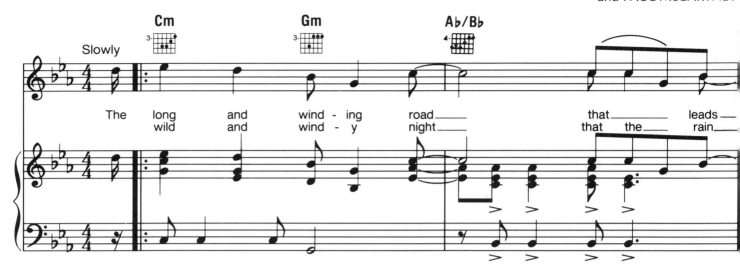

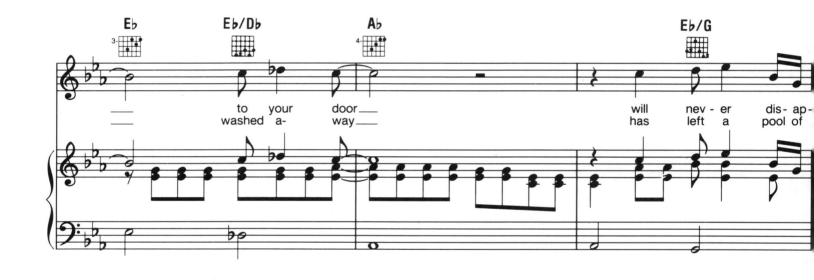

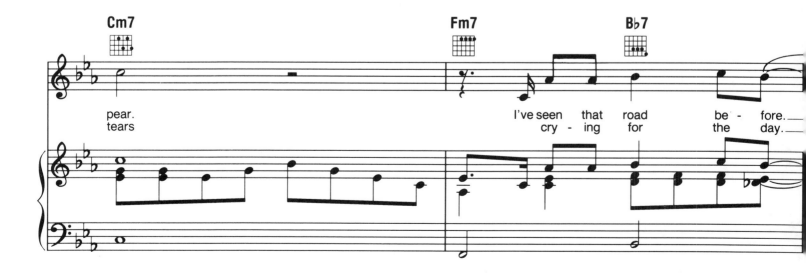

LOOK FOR THE SILVER LINING

(From "SALLY")

Words by BUDDY DeSYLVA
Music by JEROME KERN

LOVELY TO LOOK AT

(From "ROBERTA")

Words by DOROTHY FIELDS
and JIMMY McHUGH
Music by JEROME KERN

MONA LISA

(From The Paramount Picture "CAPTAIN CAREY, U.S.A.")

Words and Music by JAY LIVINGSTON
and RAY EVANS

MOON RIVER
(From The Paramount Picture "BREAKFAST AT TIFFANY'S")

Words by JOHNNY MERCER
Music by HENRY MANCINI

MOOD INDIGO

Words and Music by DUKE ELLINGTON,
IRVING MILLS and ALBANY BIGARD

You ain't been blue, ___

no, no, no. You ain't been blue, ___

___ 'til you've had ___ that mood in - di - go.

MOONLIGHT AND ROSES
(BRING MEM'RIES OF YOU)

Words and Music by BEN BLACK,
EDWIN H. LEMARE and NEIL MORET

Moderately

MOONLIGHT IN VERMONT

Words and Music by JOHN BLACKBURN
and KARL SUESSDORF

ONE VOICE

Words and Music by
BARRY MANILOW

Slowly, with much feeling

No chord

Just One Voice, _____ Sing - ing in the dark - ness, _____

_____ All it takes is One Voice, _____ Sing - ing so they

hear what's on your mind, And when you look a - round you'll find There's more than

Singing in the dark-ness,_____ All it takes is

One Voice,_____ Shout it out and let it ring._____

Just One Voice,_____ It takes that

One Voice, And ev - 'ry-

PENTHOUSE SERENADE

Words and Music by WILL JASON
and VAL BURTON

THE PARTY"S OVER
(From "BELLS ARE RINGING")

Words by BETTY COMDEN and ADOLPH GREEN
Music by JULE STYNE

PEOPLE
(From "FUNNY GIRL")

Words by BOB MERRILL
Music by JULE STYNE

PRECIOUS AND FEW

Words and Music by
WALTER D. NIMS

SACRIFICE

Words and Music by ELTON JOHN
and BERNIE TAUPIN

It's a hu-man sign when things go wrong,
Mu-tual mis-un-der-stand-ing af-ter the fact.

when the scent of her lin-gers and temp-ta-tion's strong.
Sen-si-tiv-i-ty builds a pris-on in the fi-nal act.

SAILING

Moderately (in 2)

Words and Music by
CHRISTOPHER CROSS

Well, it's not far down to par - a - dise, at least it's not for me. And if the wind is right you can sail a - way and find tran - quil - i - ty. Oh, the can -

Just a dream

Bm7　F#m9　C#m7

and the wind to car - ry me, and soon I will be free.

D(add9)　A　D.S. al Coda

Well, it's not

CODA　D(add9)

Play 3 times

R.H.

8va

SOMEWHERE OUT THERE

(From "AN AMERICAN TAIL")

Words and Music by JAMES HORNER, BARRY MANN
and CYNTHIA WEIL

through, then we'll be to - geth - er some-where out there, out where dreams come true.

SEPTEMBER SONG
(From The Musical Production "KNICKERBOCKER HOLIDAY"")

Words by MAXWELL ANDERSON
Music by KURT WEILL

241

SMOKE GETS IN YOUR EYES

(From "ROBERTA")

Words by OTTO HARBACH
Music by JEROME KERN

SOMETHING

Words and Music by
GEORGE HARRISON

Something in the way she moves,
Somewhere in her smile she knows,
Something in the way she knows,

at-tracts me like no other lov-
that I don't need no other lov-
and all I have to do is think

-er.
-er.
of her.

Something in the way she woos,
Something in her style that shows,
Something in the things she shows

SPEAK SOFTLY, LOVE (LOVE THEME)

(From The Paramount Picture "THE GODFATHER")

Words by LARRY KUSIK
Music by NINO ROTA

Speak soft-ly, love, and hold me warm a-gainst your heart. I feel your words, the ten-der, trem-bling mo-ments start. We're in a world _____ our ver-y own, shar-ing a love that on-ly few have ev-er known. Wine col-ored

STELLA BY STARLIGHT

(From The Paramount Picture "THE UNINVITED")

Words by NED WASHINGTON
Music by VICTOR YOUNG

STORMY WEATHER
(KEEPS RAININ' ALL THE TIME)

Lyrics by TED KOEHLER
Music by HAROLD ARLEN

Slow lament

THREE COINS IN THE FOUNTAIN

Words by SAMMY CAHN
Music by JULE STYNE

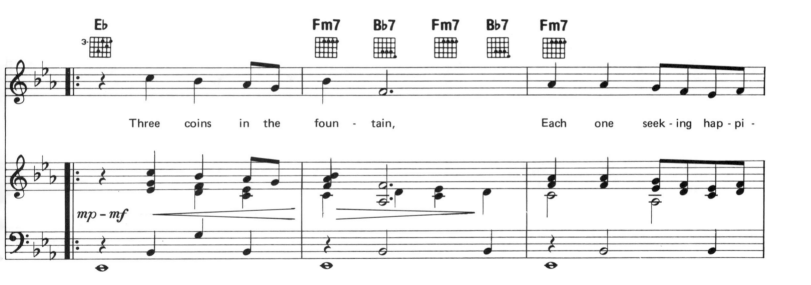

Three coins in the foun - tain, Each one seek - ing hap - pi -

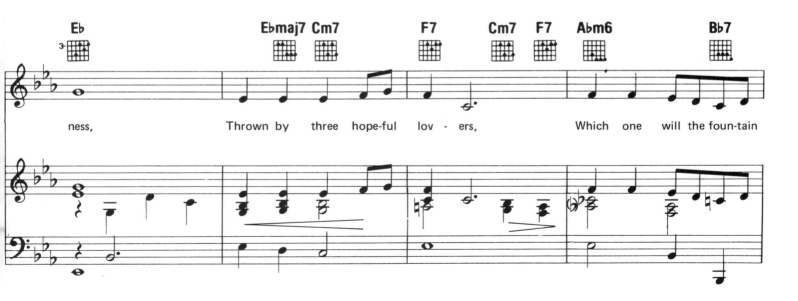

ness, Thrown by three hope-ful lov - ers, Which one will the foun-tain

TAMMY

Words and Music by RAY EVANS
and JAY LIVINGSTON

A TIME FOR US (LOVE THEME)

(From The Paramount Picture "ROMEO AND JULIET")

Words by LARRY KUSIK
and EDDIE SNYDER
Music by NINO ROTA

VINCENT (STARRY STARRY NIGHT)

Words and Music by
DON McLEAN

MCA music publishing

TO ALL THE GIRLS I'VE LOVED BEFORE

Lyric by HAL DAVID
Music by ALBERT HAMMOND

Moderately slow, with expression

THE WAY WE WERE

(From The Motion Picture "THE WAY WE WERE")

Words by ALAN and MARILYN BERGMAN
Music by MARVIN HAMLISCH

277

THE WAY YOU LOOK TONIGHT

(From "SWING TIME")

Words by DOROTHY FIELDS
Music by JEROME KERN

WHAT A DIFF'RENCE A DAY MADE

Lyric by STANLEY ADAMS
Music by MARIA GREVER

YOUNG AT HEART

(From "YOUNG AT HEART")

Words by CAROLYN LEIGH
Music by JOHNNY RICHARDS

WHAT THE WORLD NEEDS NOW IS LOVE

Lyric by HAL DAVID
Music by BURT BACHARACH

WHEN I FALL IN LOVE

Words by EDWARD HEYMAN
Music by VICTOR YOUNG

WHERE DO I BEGIN (LOVE THEME)

(From The Paramount Picture "LOVE STORY")

Words by CARL SIGMAN
Music by FRANCIS LAI

love that an-y-where I go _____ I'm nev-er

lone-ly. _____ With her a-long, _____ who could be

lone-ly? _____ I reach for her hand, _____ it's al-ways there. _____

How long does it last? _____ Can love be meas-ured by the

hours __ in a day? _____ I have no an-swers now, but this much I can say:

I know I'll need her 'til the stars all burn a - way, _____ and she'll be

there. _____

A WHOLE NEW WORLD
(ALADDIN'S THEME)

(From Walt Disney's "ALADDIN")

Music by ALAN MENKEN
Lyrics by TIM RICE